HOW? WHO? WHAT? WHEN? WHERE? WHY?

Questions kids ask

ABOUT
ANIMALS

PUBLISHER	Joseph R. DeVarennes	
PUBLICATION DIRECTOR	Kenneth H. Pearson	
ADVISORS	Roger Aubin	
	Robert Furlonger	
EDITORIAL SUPERVISOR	Jocelyn Smyth	
PRODUCTION MANAGER	Ernest Homewood	
PRODUCTION ASSISTANTS	Martine Gingras	Kathy Kishimoto
	Catherine Gordon	Peter Thomlison
CONTRIBUTORS	Alison Dickie	Nancy Prasad
	Bill Ivy	Lois Rock
	Jacqueline Kendel	Merebeth Switzer
	Anne Langdon	Dave Taylor
	Sheila Macdonald	Alison Tharen
	Susan Marshall	Donna Thomson
	Pamela Martin	Pam Young
	Colin McCance	
SENIOR EDITOR	Robin Rivers	
EDITORS	Brian Cross	Ann Martin
	Anne Louise Mahoney	Mayta Tannenbaum
PUBLICATION ADMINISTRATOR	Anna Good	
ART AND DESIGN	Richard Comely	Ronald Migliore
	George Elliott	Sue Wilkinson
	Greg Elliott	

Canadian Cataloguing in Publication Data

Questions kids ask about animals

(Questions kids ask ; 1)
ISBN 0-7172-2388-4

1. Animals—Miscellanea—Juvenile literature.
2. Children's questions and answers.   I. Comely, Richard.
II. Wilkinson, Sue.   III. Elliott, Greg.   IV. Series.

QL49.Q48 1988   j591   C88-093575-8

Questions Kids Ask... about ANIMALS

continued

Do whales have legs?

No they don't, but you may be surprised to find out that at one time they did.

Millions of years ago, the ancestors of whales had four legs and walked on land. For some reason, probably to find food, they started spending more and more time in the sea. Their bodies began to change, until they were able to live their whole life in the sea.

Instead of front legs with paws or hands, they developed flippers. We can see this by looking at the whale's skeleton. Inside each flipper are bones that look much like the bones in your arm and hand.

Further down, hidden under blubber and muscle, are the tiny bones of what were once the whale's back legs. No longer needed, they have shrunk and been absorbed into the whale's body.

TAP DANCING LESSONS upstairs

Can fish really fly?

If you sail on a tropical sea, you may come across a very strange sight—fish that appear to fly! These fish have large fins, which they push out to the side as they glide through the air. Do flying fish actually fly?

By taking pictures with high-speed cameras, scientists have found that flying fish are not really flying. True flyers, such as birds or butterflies, flap their wings when they fly. A flying fish glides without flapping, just as a kite glides through the air.

True flyer or not, a flying fish can perform some spectacular tricks. When it takes off it swims very rapidly, vibrating its tail fins to build up speed before sailing into the air. A flying fish can travel as far as 45 metres (150 feet) through the air at a speed of 55 kilometres (35 miles) per hour. Just imagine if your goldfish could do that!

Do fish sleep?

If cats take naps and kangaroos snooze, what about fish?

Like all animals, fish need to rest. They don't sleep the way we do, but they do have rest periods during which they keep very still in the water. Fish don't fall into a very deep sleep—even the slightest ripple in the water is enough to wake them up.

But a fish never looks like it's sleeping because it can't close its eyes—fish don't have any eyelids!

Many kinds of fish move their fins even when they are resting. This keeps them balanced in the water. These fish prefer to sleep without resting against something. Goldfish sleep this way.

Some fish like to sleep at the bottom of the ocean. Most kinds rest on their bellies, but triggerfish lie on their sides. Slippery dick, a fish found in coral reefs, sleeps under a sand blanket, which it makes by burrowing under the sand.

Can fish drown?

It's hard to imagine that a fish could drown. After all, fish live and breathe in water. But it is possible. Drowning means to die by suffocation in liquid. Suffocation happens when the oxygen supply to the body is cut off. People breathe oxygen from the air. They can't take oxygen from water, so if they're underwater too long they suffocate, or drown.

Fish take oxygen from water. Most fish breathe with gills, which do the same work as people's lungs. When a fish breathes, it opens its mouth and draws in a mouthful of water. The water goes down its throat, which forces it through the fish's gill openings.

If a fish's gills stop working, it can't get oxygen from the water and it suffocates. Since it is in water, it has suffocated in a liquid. So yes, you can say that fish can drown.

How many legs does a centipede have?

A centipede is a creature with one hundred legs, right? Wrong! Although it's commonly thought that all centipedes have one hundred legs, a full-grown centipede may have from fifteen to two hundred *pairs* of legs, depending on the kind of centipede it is.

A centipede's narrow, caterpillar-like body is divided into many segments, or sections. Each section has a pair of thin walking legs. Usually, a centipede grows by adding new segments, each with a new pair of legs. A few kinds are born with their full number of segments and legs.

The two front "legs" of most centipedes are actually fangs. They are connected to glands and give off a poisonous fluid that centipedes use to kill their prey— usually slugs, earthworms and insects.

The next time you see a centipede, try to count its legs. And don't be surprised if there aren't one hundred!

DID YOU KNOW . . . the largest centipede, *Scolopendra gigas*, may grow as long as 30 centimetres (12 inches). It feeds mostly on insects, but sometimes captures and eats mice and lizards!

How can you tell a butterfly from a moth?

You probably already know how to tell a butterfly from a moth. Butterflies fly around during the daylight hours. Moths are usually active at night. Also, butterflies are brightly colored while moths tend to be rather dowdy.

But can you be sure? Some moths can be seen in the daytime, and a few are brightly colored indeed. Could the butterfly you see really be a moth? Here are some other ways to tell which is which.

First of all, butterflies hold their wings erect when resting, whereas moths fold them flat against their backs. Another difference to watch for is that moths have heavier, hairier bodies, while butterflies look lighter and more delicate. A final clue is the shape of the antennae, or "feelers." A butterfly's antennae are enlarged at the tip; those of a moth are not.

How do flies walk on ceilings?

You've probably seen a fly scurrying across your ceiling. Although its body is totally upside down, it doesn't fall off.

Flies have six legs attached to the thorax, or middle section, of their bodies. Each leg has a foot. On the underside of each foot are two tiny claws. Under each claw is a hairy pad called a pulvillus. These pads are covered in a sticky, glue-like liquid. When a fly walks on the ceiling or any other surface, the pads stick or cling long enough for the fly to keep its balance. This lets flies walk upside down without falling off.

How do cats see in the dark?

A cat's round, mysterious eyes are beautiful to look at. In the dark, they seem to glow from within. But there are no lights in a cat's eyes. What makes them shine is also what helps cats to see much better in the dark than you or I.

A special layer in their eyes, called a *tapetum*, reflects extra light back into the eye when it gets dark.

So cats' eyes absorb more light in a dark room than our eyes do. This allows them to see about seven times better than people can in the dark!

How do cats purr?

Although it is still not known exactly how cats make their purring sound, it is known that all sounds are produced by vibrations. In a cat's throat vibrations occur when the major blood vessels around the vocal chords are expanded.

Unlike other animals, cats have two sets of vocal chords. One set is called the superior or false chords, and the other set is called

Why do lions roar?

Few things are more frightening than the thunderous roar of a male lion. That roar has made the lion the symbol of strength and courage for thousands of years.

Male lions don't hunt. They leave this important job to the females. The males' job is to guard the hunting area and protect the other members of the group. If an enemy tries to come too close, look out! The males ruffle up their manes, bare their sharp teeth and let go an ear-splitting roar. If they could talk they'd be shouting "GET OUT!" Their roar is usually enough to make even the bravest enemy run away.

rr...

the inferior or true chords. The true chords are responsible for a cat's various meows and cries, the false chords, for the purring.

All cats purr. Some make no sound when they purr, but you can feel the vibrations when you touch the cat's throat. Young cats purr in monotone, which means they make one continuous sound, but older cats purr on two or three notes. No matter how they do it, one thing is for certain—a purring cat is a happy cat.

Why do peacocks spread their feathers?

Some male birds sing or dance to attract a female. Others hop, peck on logs or fly zigzag across the sky. But it's the peacock who puts on the most beautiful mating show.

The best-known peacocks are the kind from India. They have a shiny greenish-blue neck and breast and a purplish-blue body. But their most remarkable feature is a long train of greenish feathers marked with bright spots that look like eyes. These feathers are about five times longer than the bird's body.

When a peacock wants to attract a female (called a peahen), he spreads his train into the shape of a huge fan and strolls slowly in front of her, hoping she will notice how handsome he is. If the peahen likes what she sees, the peacock has a new mate!

Are bald eagles really bald?

If you were to spot a group of bald eagles sitting in a tree, you would think they didn't have any feathers on their heads. Look again. They simply have white feathers on their heads that are difficult to see from a distance because they blend in with the pale

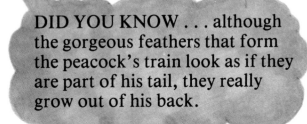

DID YOU KNOW . . . although the gorgeous feathers that form the peacock's train look as if they are part of his tail, they really grow out of his back.

color of the sky. If you do see a bald eagle with a white head, you can be sure that it is at least four years old. Until its fourth birthday, a bald eagle's head is covered with very noticeable brown feathers.

Why do woodpeckers peck?

Woodpeckers peck for a lot of reasons. Sometimes they drill into tree bark looking for ants, grubs, beetles and other insects to eat. Sometimes they bore into a tree to create a nest hole and a place to live.

But why are they often caught drumming on drain pipes, television aerials and other metal parts of your roof? After all, aren't woodpeckers supposed to peck wood?

The fact is, woodpeckers are trying to produce the loudest noise they can. They are signalling to other birds in the area that this is their territory. They are saying in effect, "I live here—you get lost!" They are also sending out invitations for a mate to come and join them.

So the next time you hear a woodpecker hammering on your roof, pay no mind. He's just trying to get his message across— and it's not for you!

Why do gorillas thump their chests?

When gorillas thump their chests, they are putting on something that scientists call a "threat display." This is something that people do, too. What it really means is not "I'm going to attack you and eat you," but rather "I don't know who you are. Keep your distance." Cats do the same thing when they hiss at you.

Gorillas are incredibly strong—a large male gorilla can easily bend thick, steel bars—but they are actually quite gentle. They rarely fight, even among themselves. They are also vegetarians, so they never eat anyone.

Can animals talk to each other?

Not the way we do. Humans are the only animals that talk to each other with words.

But animals do communicate with one another. They send messages about where to find food, about danger, mating and territory. How? Many use sounds and gestures, like we do. Mother birds and their babies call to each other to communicate their location. Cats arch their backs and spit to show anger. A rabbit warns others of danger by thumping the ground.

Animals also communicate by using their sense of touch. They prod, poke and nudge one another. Perhaps they are saying, "Get going!" Ants communicate with one another by touching their antennae.

The sense of smell is also an important means of communication. When a dog urinates on a tree, it is leaving its scent. This marks its territory and it is a signal to other dogs to stay away. Can you explain how a skunk communicates? Any idea what it's trying to say?

SQUEEK!
(TIME TO GO HOME.)

14

How do crickets chirp?

On a warm summer evening, the air comes alive with the sound of crickets singing.

Only male crickets chirp. They do this by rubbing one wing over the other. The underside of each wing has a rough, narrow strip called a file. The cricket rubs this file over a rough part, called a scraper, on the upper surface of the other wing.

The chirping sound is the cricket's mating call. The louder a cricket chirps, the more likely he is to find a mate. Male crickets often sound as if they are singing together in chorus. Each cricket is actually trying to drown out the others.

When a female appears on the scene, the male cricket's song quickly changes. A quiet, gentle song is what you will hear once he has found a mate.

Where can you see the most animals in one day?

In Tanzania, Africa, there is a national park that boasts the greatest number of animals anywhere on earth. Serengeti National Park is a wildlife refuge made up of grassland ranges, hills, swamps, lakes and forests.

Not only do many thousands of animals live year-round in the park, but every December hundreds of thousands more move in for a six-month visit.

During the first few weeks of the migration, the animals move into the eastern edge of the park. The concentration of wildlife at this spot is simply astounding:

about 700 000 animals in an area of only 4000 square kilometres (1500 square miles).

In one day in Serengeti National Park you could see wildebeest, zebras, lions, hyenas, wild dogs, giraffes, topi, jackals, cheetahs, elands, impala, buffalo, hippopotamuses, monkeys, gazelles, leopards, rhinoceroses and elephants! There is no other place else on earth where you could see so many animals in a single day.

How do birds know when to fly south?

Some birds fly, or migrate, enormous distances. For example, the tiny ruby-throated hummingbird leaves Canada in the fall and flies all the way to Central America for the winter! Then it returns to the North in the spring to lay eggs and bring up its young. How do birds know when to leave on such an incredible journey?

The answer seems to lie in the shortening fall days and the changing position of the sun. They tell the birds that winter is coming and they should fly to a warmer place where food is more plentiful. At the same time,

YIPES! I BETTER BOOK MY FLIGHT!

messengers that travel through the blood-stream, called hormones, somehow tell the bird to eat more. It needs to store up lots of energy for the long journey ahead. Some birds need one last signal to get them on their way. It could be a snowfall, or a sudden spell of cold weather which causes a drop in their food supply. When the time comes to return to the North, hormones get into the act again. They tell the reproductive organs to get ready for producing babies, and the birds get the urge to fly back to their nesting grounds.

18

Do all birds fly?

Birds have three main things in common—they lay eggs, they have wings, and they are the only animals with feathers. But, no, not all birds fly. Some birds use wings for other purposes.

Penguins spend a lot of time in the water and use their wings like flippers. Other birds, like ostriches, run or walk and use their wings only for balance. Most birds, though, do use their wings to fly: some reach speeds of well over 160 kilometres (100 miles) per hour.

Does a scarecrow really scare crows?

Farmers don't like crows because they eat sprouting corn crops. Crows are such a pest to farmers that many make scarecrows to stick in their cornfields. They hope the crows will be frightened away by the straw man, but crows are usually too clever to fall for this old trick. Crows are often seen calmly eating a corn crop while a nearby scarecrow flaps in the breeze.

Yet crows aren't bold. They are able to survive because they never take chances. When a group of crows are eating, two or three of them usually act as lookouts. Stationed on a fence post or in a tall tree, they watch for approaching farmers or other dangers. If a lookout senses danger, it will cry its loud, shrill "caw, caw." A cry of warning from one of their lookouts will send the whole flock winging away to safety.

DID YOU KNOW . . . a row of crows is called a "murder of crows."

Do coyotes chase roadrunners?

"Roadrunner, the coyote's after you. Roadrunner, if he catches you, you're through!"

No one has ever reported actually seeing a coyote chase a roadrunner, but it could happen.

Coyotes live throughout western North America and are called cunning tricksters in North American Indian lore. They are clever and can run fast enough to catch a jackrabbit. They mainly eat gophers, rats, rabbits, but will take advantage of whatever is available—including birds.

The roadrunner, which belongs to the cuckoo family, lives in the southwestern United States and northern Mexico. It earned its nickname because it rarely flies. Roadrunners prefer to run when they're frightened.

The roadrunner can run pretty fast—up to 24 kilometres (15 miles) per hour—but not as fast as a coyote. The coyote's top speed is 64 kilometres (40 miles) per hour. In a *real* race, the coyote would certainly catch the hapless roadrunner!

Beep, Beep!

Why do coyotes howl?

If you have ever spent time camping in the wild, chances are you will have heard a coyote wail. Its cry consists of yelping and howling in a sequence of high-pitched, ear-piercing moans. It is one of the most spine-tingling sounds you can imagine.

A bit of a performer, a coyote favors howling on a ridge and is especially active at dusk and dawn. One coyote howling is enough to start off an impressive mournful concert of others.

During mating season coyotes stage howling contests which often end in battle for their mates. It is thought that they howl to proclaim territory, to socialize, or even just for the sheer joy of howling. Although scientists believe coyotes have a complex system of communication, they have been unable to figure out exactly what these howls mean.

DID YOU KNOW . . . a coyote has only two weaknesses. It sleeps very heavily and it always looks back when fleeing.

Why do bees dance?

A lone bee returns home from a journey in the surrounding countryside. As soon as she enters the hive, she begins to dance. She waves, bobs and turns as the other bees cluster around her and watch. Soon the nearest bees become excited and start to dance along with her.

Sounds like fun, but there is a serious reason for this dance. Bees can't speak or write messages. Instead they use dancing as a way of "talking" to each other. The returning bee is letting the others know that she has found food.She is telling them about flowers full of sweet nectar and pollen. The movements of the dance describe the direction in which the flowers can be found, and how far away they are. The other bees copy the dancer's movements to pass the message on. Then they go off to find the food.

Instead of singing for their supper, it looks like bees would rather dance for it!

DID YOU KNOW . . . there are more ants on earth than any other insect!

ANTS UNITE

How much honey can one bee make?

Making honey is no easy task. Even though a bee's honey stomach is no bigger than a grain of rice, it may take as many as 1000 flower visits to fill it. To make just one thimbleful of honey, a single bee probably works ten hours a day for six days straight.

Being a worker bee is such hard work that most of them look scruffy by the time they are four weeks old. In the short six weeks

ALL DONE!

that most bees live a bee may produce enough honey to fill one quarter of your favorite mug.

How does an ant follow the trail of another ant?

BOB !? I THOUGHT I WAS FOLLOWING FRANK !

Have you ever seen an ant scurrying along as though it knows exactly where to go? It does—it is following a trail left for it by one of its nestmates. Ant trails are a series of scent spots left by worker ants to direct their nestmates to a food source. Special glands in the tip of the ant's abdomen produce a strong-smelling liquid. When its abdomen touches the ground, droplets are released leaving an odored trail. Other ants follow the trail by smelling the liquid with their antennae. But they must hurry. The scent trail lasts for only minutes. No wonder ants are always scurrying—they're in a hurry!

What is the largest animal that ever lived?

Did you think that the largest animal that ever lived must be some type of dinosaur? If you did, you are mistaken. The largest animal that ever lived is still alive today— the blue whale. The largest dinosaur, along with an elephant and a man, could stand on a blue whale and still have room to spare!

Blue whales can grow up to 29 metres (95 feet) long and weigh as much as 135 000 kilograms (300 000 pounds)! A newborn blue whale can be as long as 7 metres (23 feet) and weigh as much as 3 tons! That's quite a baby.

Are koalas really cuddly?

Few animals look as cute as the koala, which is found in Australia. With its large teddy-bear nose, small sad-looking eyes, big round ears and woolly gray fur, the koala looks as cuddly as can be. But koalas are not as cuddly as they look. They can be quite quick-tempered and they have long, sharp claws, which can dig deep into skin.

Koalas don't particularly want to hurt anyone. They just like to be left alone. If they are, they will happily use their claws for nothing more than climbing trees and tearing eucalyptus leaves— which are just about the only thing koalas will eat.

A koala also has strong teeth, powerful jaw muscles and a heavy body. The combination makes it a fighter to be reckoned with. Enemies such as dingos and owls usually keep their distance from adult koalas. Maybe you should too.

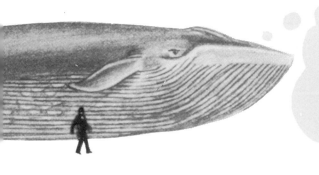

DID YOU KNOW . . . .
the blue whale grows faster than any living thing in both the plant and animal kingdoms.

Both toads and frogs are amphibians. That means they live their lives partly in water and partly on land. The adult lays eggs in the water, where they hatch. Then the baby frog or toad (called a tadpole) goes through several remarkable changes.

Both at first look more like a fish and at this stage you cannot always tell them apart. They have no legs or arms and they breathe through gills on the side of their heads. Gradually they grow limbs, their tails shrink and their gills are replaced by lungs like you have.

At this stage frogs and toads are fairly easy to tell apart. Frogs have smooth skin and (with the exception of tree frogs) spend their lives near water. Toads have warts, their skin is drier than a frog's and they are usually brown. They are land dwellers, often feeding on the worms found in gardens.

25

Do ostriches really hide their heads in the sand?

Cartoons often show a frightened ostrich burying its head in the sand as if this somehow would hide the giant bird. The ostrich would not be very smart if it really tried to hide by sticking its head in the sand, and it doesn't. So where did this story come from?

When ostriches are sitting on the nest, they do lay their long necks flat on the ground so that they are less likely to attract the attention of lions or other predators. People who saw the birds do this must have thought they were burying their heads.

If you had a neck like a flagpole, what would you do when you wanted to hide?

DID YOU KNOW . . . the smallest bird in the world is the bee hummingbird. It can be a mere 5 centimetres (2 inches) long—and about half of that is bill and tail.

Can earthworms see?

Earthworms don't have eyes, so they can't actually *see*. They do have ways of finding out about the world around them, however. They are covered in a very thin skin which can sense changes in light and temperature.

Earthworms literally feel their way around, judging where to go by what they feel through their skin. If the sun is too hot, they

Why do robins hop—then stop?

Have you ever watched a robin on the lawn? It hops —then stops, cocking its head to one side and looking at you with a bright brown eye. The robin isn't trying to be coy. It is hunting for food. Robins like to eat earthworms and have a clever way of catching them. When they hop across the grass, the patter of their tiny feet sounds, from underground, like raindrops. Earthworms come up out of the ground when it rains so that they don't drown when the rain fills their underground tunnels. After a few hops the robin stops. Nature has given it supersensitive hearing and it is listening for the soft stirrings of an earthworm. As soon as it hears the earthworm, it pokes its beak into the tiny worm hole. In a moment you'll see it pull out a long, glistening worm. Once again its trick has worked, and the hungry robin quickly flies away with its meal.

will crawl deeper into the cool soil. If the earth becomes too cold, they will crawl towards the warmth of the sun.

You may be wondering how an earthworm can find food if it can't see. The answer is that it doesn't need to see. Earthworms simply eat anything that is in front of them. They munch their way through the soil, swallowing all the dirt they can. The soil contains tiny decayed pieces of plants and animals. These are digested for food, and the dirt comes out the other end!

So the next time you see an earthworm, don't try to look it in the eye. It just doesn't have any!

Why did dinosaurs die out?

Dinosaurs first appeared about 225 million years ago. They belonged to the reptile family.

Dinosaurs ranged greatly in size. Some of them were as small as rabbits; others were the largest, most terrifying animals that every walked the earth. The biggest dinosaurs could be 27 metres (90 feet) long and could weigh more than 77 metric tons (170 000 pounds). They must have shaken the earth when they moved! Yet 65 million years ago the dinosaurs died out.

Many explanations for the disappearance of the dinosaurs have been offered. Some scientists suggest that geological changes caused the dinosaurs' vast swampland home to dry up. At the same time, temperatures became colder and the swampland plants died out. As they did so, the plant-eating dinosaurs may have gradually starved to death. When the plant-eaters died, the meat-eaters that depended on them for food also went hungry and died.

Other scientists think that disease killed off the dinosaurs or that mammals ate their eggs, and yet others that a star exploded near our solar system, generating a killing pulse of radiation. Still other scientists suggest that a huge comet or asteroid plunged into the earth from space. The resulting dust cloud circled the earth for months, creating an endless night and killing first the plants, and then the creatures that depended on them.

So far these are all just theories. We do not really know whether one, or some, or all of them can explain why the dinosaurs died out.

Does a laughing hyena really laugh?

An eerie laugh floats through the night air. It's the sound of the spotted, or laughing, hyena. But what's so funny? The hyena didn't just hear a good joke.

The noise a hyena makes is a mixture of a strange growl and a gurgle. It just happens to sound to us like laughter. Hyenas make these sounds when they're prowling for food or when they get excited.

It would be a bad mistake to think that just because hyenas laugh, they are friendly. They can weigh as much as 80 kilograms (175 pounds), and have jaws so strong that they can crush and eat large bones. Laughing hyenas are no laughing matter. But don't worry—they are only found in Africa and India.

Do all mosquitos bite?

You may think that all mosquitos bite. After all, how many have you met that didn't? In fact, only the females do. Male mosquitos have a short beak which they use to suck plant juices for food. Females have a long, slender beak which they use to pierce the skin of birds, animals and, of course, humans.

The females suck blood from their victims because they need it to nourish their eggs. You may not like the idea, but it's all part of being a good mosquito mother.

Can crabs climb trees?

You are lying on the beach of a tropical island watching the waves lap lazily against the shore. All of a sudden a crab scampers— not on the sand but up a tree! What kind of crab is this?

On many tropical islands lives a tree-climbing crab called the Coconut Crab. A Coconut Crab can grow as long as 60 centimetres (two feet). It lives in burrows, which it digs beneath the palms. When it gets hungry, the Coconut Crab jumps out of its burrow, climbs the palm and picks a fresh coconut. It cracks the coconut open with its powerful front claws and feasts on the sweet coconut meat.

So don't be surprised if you're on a tropical island and look up to see crabs in the trees!

Why do skunks smell?

As many of us know to our sorrow, skunks may be small but their smell is mighty!

Skunks have special glands at the base of their bushy tails which hold a yellowish, foul-smelling fluid called musk. If a skunk is frightened or in danger it will lift its tail and spray by squeezing strong muscles that force the musk out. It can squirt as far as 4 metres (12 feet), and the smell will linger for hours!

A skunk will usually give a warning that it's about to spray by stamping its front paws and hissing or growling. The skunk's spray is its only natural defense, so if the attacker doesn't run when the skunk hisses, look out! In a split second the air will be filled with the unforgettable odor of skunk!

WALK SOFTLY... CARRY A BIG STINK!

How does a snake shed its skin?

Shortly after a snake hatches from its egg, it sheds its skin. It doesn't shed its entire skin, just the thin outermost layer. It will repeat this process from time to time for the rest of its life.

Why does it do this? For the same reason that you must get new clothes from time to time—you outgrow the old ones. And though a snake grows larger too, its outer layer of skin does not grow with it. When it's time to shed, the skin grows dull and tight. The snake then rubs its nose against a hard, rough surface like a rock or tree trunk to loosen the old skin around its lips. When the old skin begins to break away, the snake snags the loose part on a rock or twig. Then the snake slides out of the old skin through the mouth opening. It leaves the old skin in one piece, turned inside out, and emerges in a shiny new skin that has grown under the old one. The entire process takes only a few minutes.

Index